Precious Asses

*To my old friend
the biographical fallacy
and the names taken in vain herein
with appreciation*

Precious Asses

Loosely from the Latin of Gaius Valerius Catullus of Verona

James Methven

Winner of the 2009 *Poetry Wales* Purple Moose Prize

SEREN

Seren is the book imprint of
Poetry Wales Press Ltd.
57 Nolton Street, Bridgend, Wales, CF31 3AE
www.seren-books.com

© James Methven, 2009

ISBN 978-1-85411-532-4

A CIP record for this title is available from the British Library.

All rights reserved. No part of this publication may be reproduced,
stored in a retrieval system, or transmitted at any time or by any means,
electronic, mechanical, photocopying, recording or otherwise without
the prior permission of the copyright holder.

Printed in Bembo by W.O. Jones, Ltd., Llangefni.

Poetry Wales gratefully acknowledges the sponsorship
of Purple Moose Brewery, Porthmadog. **www.purplemoose.co.uk**

Contents

Lip service	7
Bean counters	8
Kiss-o-gram kiss-a-thon	9
Endurance test	10
He steals napkins	11
Bigger *IS* better	12
For your eyes only	13
"Thank God I'm normal"	15
The lessons of youth	16
"So what?"	17
August at the lido	18
"This year's crop of kisses"	19
Obsession	20
Get on with it	21
All you can eat for £5.99	22
Bag lady	23
Some grit in the oyster	24
Handsome is as handsome does	25
All eyes	26
Hard copy	27
On beauty	28
Special to me	29
A family affair	30
Girls and boys	31
Hard to say	32
Royal Bank of Methven	33
Generation Facebook	34
On 'Translation'	35
Author Note	36
Index on Catullus	37

Lip service

Who's going to want this dedicated to him,
My brand new collection, all scrubbed up nicely?
You, Jonny – at Rhodz' 21st you thought
My chat worth soaking up, and boldly
Swapped stories of Latin lovers:
Right shite come-ons 'bout locker-room fun
And, Jesus, you played at being intelligent,
Which did my head in. Anyway, joking aside,
I'm yours, I'm still waiting; you can have me
Any which way, and this trashy book, should you wish –
O you great big virgin, let's hope you're worth it.

(PS Jonny, if you're reading this, give us a call.)

Bean counters

Nell, loving you's worth living for,
C'mon – let's escape these old boys' chatter,
Puritan thoughts ain't worth a penny.
The sun sets, yes, but, you know, it comes back;
We've got one chance only, one night's span –
Mmmm? Sleep wasn't what I had in mind.
Give us a kiss, a thousand circling it, a hundred on top of them,
Here's room – just! – for another thousand, a second hundred *here*,
Space for a further thousand over *here*, *here's* where you can plant the next hundred,
Till we've spent millions and more, kissed to our limits,
I'm not worried about our figures: screw them!
We'll bore accountants and peeping toms, do
Quadratic equations with our tongues –
Hang on, I've lost count: can we start again?

Kiss-o-gram kiss-a-thon

Since you're asking, Andy, where I'd draw the line
On kiss-kiss-kissing you, here's my hopeless answer:
I'd smooch you as often as the waves lick the shore
At Frinton – cold brine sucks nipples –
I'd tongue you all the way round from where
Your – Birthday Boy – "shrine" stands tall as God's to where
Your – Batty Boy – "sacred sepulchre" darkly sweats:
As many kisses as there are stars winking
At our silent nights made noisy with
Your furtive manly delving:
Kiss-hungry – I'd be
        Kiss-slaked – you'd be
                Kiss-maddened – we'd be
                        Saliva-slicked with
Too many kisses for the bi-curious to count
Too many kisses for the loose-tongued to jaw.

Endurance test

Gutted, Jimmy, give over clowning,
And what you know is dead, leave so.
In dreams the sun tans me blondly meek,
Puppy stumbling wherever my girl strings me,
Loving her like we ain't loving no-one no more,
A blissful time of silly sentiment,
When you said 'Yes', and she never said 'No':
Without knowing, I let the sun bleach me white.
Now she don't want it, you too stop wanting it, not
Chase what splits, nor live in tears,
But with mind made cruel, endure.
Here's goodbye. See your Jimmy endure,
Ain't going to beg, ain't going to ask at all.
Hush your grieving when no-one comes calling.
You lovely bitch, what life's yours?
Who now visit you? Deem you fair?
Be loved by you? Call you his?
Be kissed by you? Bite your lips? Who?
Ah, you, Jimmy, destitute, endure.

He steals napkins

Mauro, you inelegant man, that's no pretty use
Of the left fist, deep in the jokes and wine:
Light-fingering linen from unguarded crotches.
You call this 'sassy'? You're way off, asshole:
In word and deed, it's sordid and plain wrong.
You don't believe me? Go see Lee, your brother,
He'd re-mortgage that swish new Chelsea pad
To hush your thievery; he knows what's what.
So either hand it back – ring 'n all; come on – or expect the full
Broadside, a royal flush of my crudest satirical verses. And
Don't think I'm moved by some guff about cost, I care 'coz
It's a souvenir from two old students, friends, who
Scored these dainty napkins while in Spain, did
Freddy and Will. I'm bound to love them just as much
As I ever did my willing Will and ready Freddy.

Bigger *IS* better

You'll dine royally, Fred, chez moi,
In – Insha'Allah – a few days' time: just call in:
So long as you shell for a right royal
Feast, not forgetting the obligat'ry blonde
And the wine and the salt and the freshest gags.
If, I say, you schlep these in, *caro mio*,
You'll eat well, coz your Jimmy's
Wallet is – temp'ra'ly – all moths.
But I'll defray your costs with undiluted love
Or whatever's suaver, more chi-chi:
I'll perfume the air with that scent
Heaven lent my Nell, Venus' sweat,
And when you sniff it, God you'll ask
To bless you, Freddy, in one vast nose.

For your eyes only

Dear Alan,

In haste, am heading Londonwards at short notice.
I leave amber-curled Kyle in your glamour-boy hands –
Is this wise? Kyle – who's every kiss I've ever kissed.
This modest request only I ask of you: for all the frets you've fretted
To know your love's true and faithful while you're out of town,
Leave unpicked my boy's cherry, and, should the two of you pop out
To the pool, say, or for some food, or – wince – a club, keep him safe,
Watch out for the lads who strut the High, the Broad, Carfax, and the Turl,
Identikit-clothed, all bent on trouble, all out for fun, all lads together:
Warn them off. Thanks a lot for doing this. I owe you.

See over.

Mind, what I fear more is your famed shire-horse schlong,
That's been slapped for a laugh on all the team's mobiles
Pulping whole kilos of ripe cherries of boys both curious and innocent.
Look, shoot your weapon of mass destruction where you will, as you will,
Brandish it at other boys of any age, expose it in all weathers for all I care,
But for old love's sake make my love the exception. Now,
Should your cock-crazed sphincter-sick bum-sex-obsessed mentality
Goad you to pull off the greatest crime of all – betrayal –
Here's my warning fairly given: I'll stake you in the quad, for all to see,
Face-down, arms bound, and legs stretched wide wide wide apart
It'll be time for your arse-hole to say, 'Hello!' to Mr Radish and Mr Mullet-Fin.

Yours ever,

Jimmy D

"Thank God I'm normal"

I'll shaft you arse and throat,
Alan and Kris, pathetic passives both,
What, you think 'coz I translate Catullus thus
That I'm a perv? Oh! come on, puh-lease!

I'll grant some schools of thought
Picture the poet's "life" as nestlé demure,
And howl should "arse" and "tit" feature in it:
Great biographical fallacies are
Well wrapped round their necks,
They haven't a clue how to dish up the sex,
    Ears of tin, mouths not fit
      To let the fragrant sauce slide in,
I'm shrimping for words here in these verses,
To raise more than a smile, a rush of blush:
I'm speaking to the elderly, not the already heated young,
Some verbal viagra for the grey-rinse crowd
To get their nursing-homied stiff loins
Stiffied up.

So here's to you, Alan and Kris!
Thank God you're dumb enough to eye
My "thousand sloppy kisses" and think me queer.

As I said. Arse. *Then* mouth. Both of you. Enjoy.

The lessons of youth

Kyle – O! – best bearer of that name, now,
Everpast, evermore, till poets tire, and words
No longer ink the flesh of youth, I'd rather you
Give all of Midas' riches to he whose
Niggard wealth lacks chat and means,
Than spend your golden love on him.
'What, isn't he a nice guy?' I hear you say.
Yeah. Nice. Sure. But Mr Niceguy's niceness
Can't disguise – dress it up, down, or how you will –
He's without chat and wherewithal.

"So what?"

Cherie dear, your cute bob *is* lovely,
    Mind, at that price it should be,
Tho' I must say it leaves your neck
    Looking a little draughty.

Blown to the East, tugged to the West,
    Nuzzled to the South, Northwards floating:
Cherie's immaculate hair
    Wins our hearts and votes.

The other thing you prob'ly don't want to hear,
    Sweet Cherie, is this: when your hubby
Talks of 'homeland security', he's not referring
    To your quim-stretching mortgage.

    Horrid child, thus to swear,
    At Cherie's immaculate hair.

August at the lido

Best of all the locker-room thieves are
Sugar-daddy Jez and his Calvin-clad 'son',
For, if Jezza's hand is the more rapacious,
Calvin-boy's *culo* is the more capacious.
Why don't the two of you fuck off on your holidays
To some sewage-slicked shore? 'Coz, Jez, trust me,
Ev'rybody knows about your sticky fingers, and,
As for that hairy arse of yours, sonny,
You're gonna have to sugar wax it,
If you wanna make any money.

"This year's crop of kisses"

Kyle, those honey-flecked eyes of yours,
    Drown in honey;
That honey-suckled smile of yours,
    Tastes of honey;
That honey-combed hair of yours,
    Smells of honey;
I lose track of the times I sucked the honey
    From your syrup body, licked the honey
From your treacle chest, from off those nectar lips
    That bees delight to sting and swell:

Let's say a round three hundred thousand

    – Around three hundred thousand –

It's not enough. My sweet tooth's hunger's up.
    Crop all the grain the world can grow,
Thresh it, thrash it, lash it, mash it, count it one by one,

    Then

Tell me how many honey-dew ripe kisses
    Your honeysome body still can bear.

Obsession

How does it go?

To me that man is God,
More than God – God willing – ,
Who sits facing her, eyes her, ears her
    Careless

Laughter. Seeing this, a sensual hell guts me;
Just so, for when I light on you, Nell,
There's nothing left of my voice –
    My poet's words –

My practised tongue glues, my skin
Thrills with melting fire, my ears
Drown in thicked deep-sea noise, my eyes
    Flare dark and dazzle out.

Time on your hands, Jimmy, that's your problem:
Time's your guilty joy, stretched idleness your life and work:
Time, that humbles kings and rubbles cities whole
    To dust.

Get on with it

Why bother, Jim? Why this procrastination?
Your old 'I want to die' routine is wearing thin.
A nonentity squats – 's blocked sphincter frenching air –
Straining the chairman's brown-stained stool;
Some hoorayed whore lies publicly in office:
Why bother, Jim? Embrace the ferry-man.

All you can eat for £5.99

Rhodz, I thought you should know:
Your Phoebe, my Phoebe, that Phoebe
    Whom – uniquely –
Your Jimmy loved more than
All the boys and girls he's ever loved –
Was last seen in the door of that greazy
Chinese 'Eat as Much as You Like' caff,
Chowing down on the 'skins of
High-minded hoodied chavs.

Bag lady

Saucy Bolognese, Rufa, sucks Rufus's meaty balls
(Tho' she's married to God knows who).
    That's not all –
She's often to be seen in cemeteries,
Stealing the floral tributes.
Look! – 'nother singed plastic 'mum is hers,
Wrestled from the undertaker's half-clipped 'prentice boy
At the crem's death-sooted doors.

Some grit in the oyster

He said he'd rather wake with me than anyone,
    Even God, supposing He were up for it.
That's what he said: but, what a young lad mouths
    To the man who wants him, should be written on the wind,
Pissed away as so much water.

Handsome is as handsome does

Isn't Neil a pretty boy; boy, ain't he just! Nell loves him
    Straight down the line – certainly more than she loves you,
Jimmy, and all your "hopeless" kind who won't make up their mind.
    Still, that Nell should love Neil stands to reason, since her
Narcissus love is mirrored in his face, his hair, his eyes, hers.
    But find me three of Mr Pretty's friends who'll shake his hand,
Or slap his back, or kiss his cheeks, and I'll show you three
    Thorough-going pretty shits shitting pretty.

All eyes

Joe, if you want Jim to swap eyes with you
    Or whatever's more him than his eyes,
Don't thieve from him, what's much more to him
    Than eyes, or, again, more him than his eyes.

Hard copy

Hate. Love. And *you* have to ask me why.
 I don't know. I feel it burning up my spine.
~~I can't~~
 ~~I can't~~

There's your answer.

On beauty

Pretty Polly wins vox pop for beauty queen; I grant you
She's blonde and she's dainty tall and she stands up straight.
Yes, I'll grudge you these individual points of beauty. Yawn.
    As for beautiful, no, that I can't allow,
        For she has no — what's the word — Venusery in her veins:
No magic, no spice, no salt-lick sweat to deck her delicate white skin.
    Why, she'd snap if you touched her.
Now, Nell *is* beautiful, for, besides that she embodies beauty,
The bold girl has climbed the Venusberg and stolen all —
    Even Venus pouts pale by comparison.

Special to me

No woman can claim she's been loved as truly madly
    Deeply – truly – 's deeply as Nell's been loved by me.
No bound ally in tight pass found fidelity come
    So often to relieve so hard a situation.

A family affair

Whose bright idea was it, Geth, to throw a nude pyjama party?
    Yours? Your mum's? Your sister's?
Likewise, d' you imagine the editor of *Incest Monthly*,
    'd be giving you the old thumbs up,
When you jazzed in your uncle's bed?

Have you no shame? Let me tell you, Geth,
    It'll take more than those great foam-daddies,
The Pacific and Atlantic, to sluice your column clean,
    And that party trick – where you bend right over
And mouth saliva down its length – doesn't count.

Girls and boys

What's this?

'Joe 4 Luke' 'Joe 4 Lucy' –
Oh, I see: Joe and Joe, flat mates,
– Two of Oxford's brightest –
Have decorated their shaving mirror
With the names of those cute twins
They pulled last night. Well,
Here's a nice new riff
On that sweet old phrase
"the brotherhood of man".

What can I add to the misted glass?

My finger's here for you, Joe,
For we've been through it all
Together. You endured my
Spoony moody puppy passion,
And dealt kindly with my feelings –
Ha! "Feelings" – that time
I got a boner. Anyway.
Joe, give him one from me.

Hard to say

Through how many borders and by how many unknown sea-stretches
    I am here, brother, to pay on this strand for which you fought
My civilian dues to your last rest. See, I have brought our parents' stone
    – a simple thing, it speaks plainly of your goodness –
They could not come themselves, being too old, too … , too broken
    By your death. Here. Your sand-mulched ashes do not speak,
As in life we are too dusty silent. How did I expect it else?
    Brother, here I am, weeping, on this foreign shore
For you, first born and dead first; our parents' memento,
    And these, my careful words, now wetted
With unaccustomed tears – there is only boyhood's ritual
    To help me. We learnt it together. And so, in your shadow, I say it:
Brother, for always, hello and your famous short b'bye.

Royal Bank of Methven

Garrad, I'd quite like back that fifty quid I 'loaned'
    To save your unwashed unshaved bacon,
All gap-year motor-mouth and cheeky charm;

        "Oh, I was mugged"
        "Oh, they had knives"
        "Oh, I was drugged"
        "Oh – " I was taken for a ride;

Sure, if you like taking money off strangers, keep it,
    Tart, but since your M.O. is here writ large,
You'll need another way to make mouth and
    Cheek earn you passage round the world.

Generation Facebook

Rhodz, you filthy sinner, when Jimmy first accessed Facebook,
    Sophia had two regulars in her intimate circle.
But now he's joined the ruddy thing, you'd have to cleft
    Each one a thousand times, so quick is friendship's siren's ring.

On 'translation'

Translation is a word used here to cover a variety of sins. Admittedly, without a first-century BC poet from Verona who lived in Rome at the time of Caesar, my poems could not be. Those, however, who can read Latin will perceive (and those who can't would soon work out) that while some of these versions lie relatively close to any accepted idea of translation, many are appropriations, fantasias, or games. The poems found their voice once I decided on a major departure from past translation practice: the substitution on the page of a version of my name for that of Catullus, for I reasoned that if he, as author, placed himself dramatically in his poems, and ran the risk of being misconstrued biographically in his self-exposure (he deals with this literary thorn in poem no. 16), then I was duty bound to do the same if the energy of the originals were to be communicated; to translate the Latin in to a modish version of modern English while leaving an obviously dead Roman name on the page didn't work. Similarly, by a process of shuffling which gathered its own momentum, the Roman chief god, Jupiter, came out as God, Caesar morphed to the PM, and a range of cultural references and language choices in the originals are here transmogrified. Catullus's Lesbia becomes my Nell, his Juventius my Kyle, and a cast list of modern names applied for their sounds and associations. Where Catullus makes use of vocabulary with a foreign (Greek) flavour or etymology I have imported (though not necessarily in direct substitution) snippets of French or Italian, or other voices that use English. Some flavour of the originals survives in mutated form in these encounters and exchanges between twenty-first-century English and a voice whose historic moment is physically lost to us.

My thanks are due to my Latin teachers from various points in my education: John Winstanley and Donald Moss of STRS in Gloucester, and in memory of Leighton Reynolds of BNC, Oxford – none of whom could have predicted the havoc here wrought. Any errors in eliciting the nuances of the Latin are my own.

JCM

Author Note

James Methven was born in Exeter to Scottish and Irish parents and grew up in Greenock on the coast of the Clyde in Scotland, before moving to Gloucester for his teenage years. He read Classics and English at Brasenose College, Oxford. After teaching English and rugby for several years at Fyling Hall School in Robin Hood's Bay in North Yorkshire he returned to take a doctorate in Victorian literature at Oxford. Since 1999 he has been working as a Lecturer in English at Oriel College. He researches and lectures on Victorian Gothic, dirt in literature, and modern theatre (which he also directs). He first encountered Catullus aged fifteen in school, though the translations he achieved for 'O' level were rather different from the ones published here. He worked on *Precious Asses* while travelling to Essaouira in Morocco, the Loire valley in France, and Sennen Cove in Cornwall, and polished the poems in various Oxford coffee shops and his study at College. This is his debut volume of poetry.

Index

Lip service –
Catullus no. 1 (cui dono lepidum novum libellum)

Bean counters –
Catullus no. 5 (vivamus, mea Lesbia, atque amemus)

Kiss-o-gram kiss-a-thon –
Catullus no. 7 (quaeris, quot mihi basiationes)

Endurance test –
Catullus no. 8 (miser Catulle, desinas ineptire)

He steals napkins –
Catullus no. 12 (Marrucine Asini, manu sinistra)

Bigger IS better –
Catullus no. 13 (cenabis bene, mi Fabulle, apud me)

For your eyes only
Catullus no. 15 (Commendo tibi me ac meos amores)

"Thank God I'm normal" –
Catullus no. 16 (pedicabo ego vos et irrumabo)

The lessons of youth –
Catullus no. 24 (o qui flosculus es Iuventiorum)

"So what?" –
Catullus no. 26 (Furi, villula vestra non ad Austri)

August at the lido –
Catullus no. 33 (o furum optime balneariorum)

"This year's crop of kisses" –
Catullus no. 48 (mellitos oculos tuos, Iuventi)

Obsession –
Catullus no. 51 (ille mi par esse deo)

Get on with it –
Catullus no. 52 (quid est, Catulle?)

All you can eat for £5.99 –
Catullus no. 58 (Caeli, Lesbia nostra, Lesbia illa)

Bag lady –
Catullus no. 59 (bononiensis Rufa Rufulum fellat)

Some grit in the oyster –
Catullus no. 70 (nulli se dicit)

Handsome is as handsome does –
Catullus no. 79 (Lesbius est pulcer; quid ni?)

All eyes –
Catullus no. 82 (Quinti, si tibi vis oculos debere Catullum)

Hard copy –
Catullus no. 85 (odi et amo)

On beauty –
Catullus no. 86 (Quintia formosast multis)

Special to me –
Catullus poem no. 87 (nulla potest mulier tantum se dicere amatam)

A family affair –
Catullus no. 88 (quid facit is, Gelli)

Girls and boys –
Catullus no. 100 (Caelius Aufillenum et Quintius Aufillenam)

Hard to say –
Catullus no. 101 (multas per gentes)

Royal Bank of Methven –
Catullus no. 103 (aut, sodes, mihi redde decem sestertia, Silo)

Generation Facebook –
Catullus no. 113 (Consule Pompeio primum duo, Cinna)